LOVE POEMS

BY

TWO INSENSITIVE GUYS

Published by
ROUND ABOUT PRESS
P.O. Box 10712
White Bear Lake, Mn 55110
(612)653-8064

Library of Congress Catalog Card Number: 91-62537
ISBN 0-9630219-0-7

Printed and bound in the United States of America.

# LOVE POEMS

# BY

# TWO INSENSITIVE GUYS

**Written by Karl J. Olson
and
Kelly M. Greenwood**

**Photos by Larry L. Aus**

# ACKNOWLEDGMENT

The *three* of us, who put this book together, would like to thank the people that helped us with inspiration, photos, and moral support.

They are: Jennifer Ziegahn, Jean Aus, and Carol Bottoni for their inspiration, Sheila Machacek and Luanne Lippold for editing and Tom Taylor for the computer support. We would also like to thank our parents, Stanton and Arline Olson and Harry and Ruth Greenwood for the photos of us as two young insensitive boys!

Last but not least, we would like to thank **all the women we *loved?* before!**

# INTRODUCTION

We would not be honest if we let you believe
that this book was written by two insensitive
guys. It was, in fact, written over a ten year
period, by two average guys. We, at the first
printing of the book, are in our late 30's and
early 40's. We have had many relationships
and have been married and divorced at least
once. This book contains a collection of poems
that we wrote about our relationships.

The poems have been arranged in a manner
that tells the story of what we go through in
the life cycle of relationships. It does not
necessarily mean that these poems were
written in the order that they appear.

The point that we are making with this book
is that men do in fact have feelings, and many
times we are the more sensitive ones in
relationships. But, we are also the ones who
quite often have problems expressing our
feelings and need some form of outlet to get
them across. Also, we will be the first to
admit that we are, in some cases, the victims
of our own insensitive actions, like so many
other men.

*Larry*

# CONTENTS

CHAPTER ONE

# THE PERSONALS

*Kelly*

# THE VERY PERSONALS

Kinda nice,
Kinda shy,
Kinda handsome,
Kinda guy.

Seeking someone,
Kinda sweet,
Kinda pretty,
Kinda neat.

If this is you,
Kindly reply,
Cause I may be
Your kinda guy.

*Kelly*

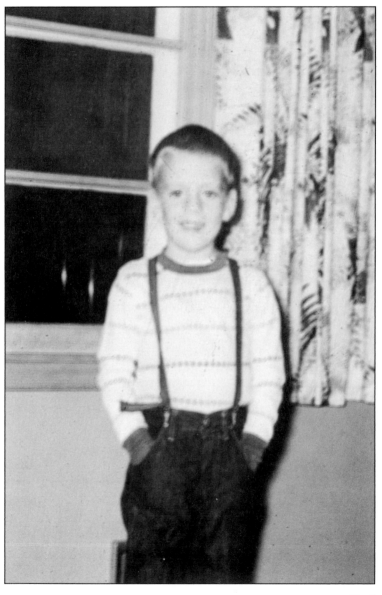

*Karl*

# GIVE ME A RING

A little crazy,
A little wild,
A lot of humor,
But a little mild.

A little weather,
It's nature's call.
A walk in leaves,
It's in the fall.

Love the music,
Love to dance,
Some conversation,
Some light romance.

If this verse
You'd like to sing,
Pick up the phone,
Give me a ring.

*Karl*

# WOULD YOU LIKE?

Would you like
>  the feeling of jumping out of an airplane
>  flying through the air and dropping
>  rapidly through space?

Would you like
>  the numbing sound of the battering wind
>  pounding your face, pulling your hair,
>  and ripping at your clothes?

Would you like
>  to close your eyes, let your thoughts go,
>  and totally blank out your mind
>  to magnify and savor this sensation?

Would you like
>  to look me up, take my hand,
>  and free fall through life
>  an evening at a time?

Would you like
>  my number?

*Karl*

# TO LOVE

To love a hateful person
    will freeze your very soul
    will bring a violent ending
        as you strive to reach your goal.


To love a selfish person
    will destroy your very essence
    will deliver so much anguish
        your life will have no presence.


To love a thoughtless person
    will consume your energy
    will show you such an awful time
        that you'll just want to be.

To love a sharing person
    will bring you much reward
    will satisfy your wants and needs
        yet still you might get bored.


To love a caring person
    will help secure your hope
    will assist you through your problems
        and guide you down life's slope.


To love a loving person
    will warm your inner soul
    will fill your years with happiness
        and make your life more whole.


*Karl*

I *know* you're out there somewhere!

CHAPTER TWO

# DATING

# WHIMSICAL NIGHTS

A thought, a dream,
A poem, a scheme;
A vision in the night.

A laugh, a cry,
A smile, a sigh;
To you in rhymes I'll write.

*Kelly*

# TOGETHER

Like a flower
    and a bee,
We're symbiotic
    you and me.

Like the ocean
    and the sand,
We'll flow through life,
    hand in hand.

Like a mountain
    with its pine,
I'll be yours,
    and you'll be mine.

*Kelly*


# YEAR AFTER YEAR

Summer treads
    the silver shore
And opens into
    Autumn's door.
Winter catches it
    on the reef
And holds it in
    its frozen sheath.
Spring will melt
    the crystal rain
And summer soon
    is back again.

*Kelly*

# ONCE AGAIN

Once again I look at you
    and my problems go away.
Thoughts of you give me strength
    and I can face the day.

Once again I hear from you
    and I begin to melt.
If I could put it all in words
    I would tell you how I felt.

Once again I look at you
    and I straighten up my spine.
I want to go and show you off
    and brag that you are mine.

Once again I am with you
    and both my knees get weak.
I want to hold you in my arms
    and slow dance, cheek to cheek.

*Karl*

# AND THERE YOU WERE

My life was a little empty
      it seemed a little blue.
I knew I needed something -
      that was all so true.

I did a lot of searching
      I gave it all I had.
I didn't know what it was -
      it made me very sad.

Then I gave up searching
      I was tired, that's for sure.
So then I just lived my life -
      and WOW, there you were!

*Karl*

# IT

It draws my attention
    from my own inner being.
It leaves me a vision
    without even seeing.

It gnaws, it nags,
    it won't leave me alone.
It grates me all over
    right down to the bone.

It comes from nowhere,
    this god-awful quest.
It stays for long hours,
    it gives me no rest.

It drags out my evenings
    into the next day.
It is wanting you,
    all of you, all the way.

*Karl*

# OH YES!

Oh, the stiffness,
     a leg in a cast
Yes, the relief,
     again running fast.

Oh, the pain,
     head banging the wall
Yes, the relief,
     stopped, in spite of it all.

Oh, the weight,
     roof covered with ice
Yes, the relief,
     all melted so nice.

Oh, the pressure,
     from earth's outer crust
Yes, the relief,
     spurts lava, it must.

Oh, the anguish,
     as I have just said
Yes, the relief,
     with you in my head.

*Karl*

# HOT

What is it
>     that corrals my attention,
>     and forces me to concentrate so intensely?

What is it
>     that brings you into focus so sharply
>     while blurring everything else in sight?

What is it
>     that makes your whispers loud and clear
>     as they penetrate all other noise?

What is it
>     that gives me the desire to grab you,
>     and take you, right here, right now?

What is it
>     that causes me to want you
>     so god damn bad?

*Karl*

# CHAPTER THREE

# FALLING IN LOVE

# FEAR

I dreamed
      I was a trapeze artist
      flying through the air
      for the first time,
            without a safety net.

I dreamed
      I was a standing in the middle
      of a very large crowd
      with everybody staring at me,
            I was naked.

I dreamed
      I told her I love her.

*Karl*

# WHAT SENSE IS THIS?

What sense is this?
One cannot see love,
    but I envision it.
One cannot smell love,
    but the aroma is in the air.

What sense is this?
One cannot hear nor taste love,
    but I imagine it.
One cannot touch love,
    but I feel it so strong!

What sense is this?
One cannot see, taste, nor smell love,
    but I do.
One cannot hear nor touch love,
    but I do all of these things.

What sense is this?
I can see you
    when you are not here.
I can hear you
    when you are quiet.
I can taste and smell you
    when I am alone.
And I can feel you
    without a touch.

*Karl*

# COMPARE

Compare if you're sly
    the grains of sand
        that on earth's shores lie
    to the tiny stars
        that line the sky
    to the number of times
        I've wished you nearby.

Compare if you will
    the drops of water
        that of oceans fill
    to the beads of dew
        from early morn chill
    to the tears of joy
        which for you I spill.

Compare at your leisure
    the comforts of home
        that you might pleasure
    to riches of man
        that total all treasure
    to my love for you
        that one can not measure.

*Karl*

# WHEN

When I think of you
    you saturate my mind
I dream of being with you
I dream of holding you
I dream of loving you.

When I am with you
    I forget about time
My clock stops ticking
My hours turn into moments
My schedules become worthless.

When I am holding you
    the world is at peace
All the nations become allies
All needs and wants are fulfilled
All of nature sings in harmony.

When I make love to you
    I have no past
Each breath is a new experience
Each touch is a new sensation
Each second is a new beginning.

*Karl*

# EVERY SEASON

When the days are short
    and the Winter cold is here,
I will be there to hold you close
    and keep you warm, my dear.

When the Spring approaches
    and the birds begin to sing,
To keep you happy and content
    I will do anything.

In the heat of summer
    when the blazing sun gods rule,
I'll turn the air conditioner on
    to keep you nice and cool.

And as the Summer turns
    into Autumn crisp and bright,
I'll be there and helping you
    make everything all right.

*Kelly*

# ALL MY LOVE

I can't give you a fairy tale
    or a castle on a hill.
I don't have the riches of the world
    and I never will.

The only thing I have to give,
    for all the world to see,
Is all my love for all my life
    until eternity.

*Kelly*

# IMAGINE THIS

Imagine a mighty majestic lion
lying on his favorite sun-warmed boulder
with his belly full and his hunger quenched.

Imagine the size and awesome strength
of his powerful legs, neck, and jaw
that he uses only to survive.

Imagine him with his head erect
as he calmly scans his kingdom
with his mate and offspring in plain view.

Imagine his feeling of being ruler
with such great confidence,
not having to prove his authority.




Imagine how happy and content
this mighty beast would be at this
very moment in his life in the jungle.




Imagine this is how you make me feel
when we are lying together
and I am holding you in my arms.


*Karl*

# DAILY DIARY

As the sun
    awakens me in the morning,
    my head is in a fog
    and my thoughts unclear,
        like far-away mountains
        fading through the distant haze.


As the sun
    reaches its peak in the sky,
    many thoughts enter and leave me
    with few staying long,
        like thousands of honey bees
        swarming the busy hive.


As the sun
    hangs high above the western horizon,
    one pleasant thought lingers
    with an aura of lightness,
        like swaying on a porch swing
        in the cool country air.

As the sun
> gives way to the darkness,
> the thought dominates my mind,
> my every moment,
>> like a newborn child
>> overwhelming a first time father.


As the moon
> peeks through my bedroom window,
> I crave to hold you in my arms
> and lie next to you,
>> like I have done
>> so many times before.

*Karl*

# WHISPER

I'm not a king of rhetoric,
     nor a preacher on a hill.
I don't shout my words from peach crates
     and I never will.

The only things I have to say
     I'll whisper in your ear.
Like: my dear sweet babe I love you,
     and it's nice to have you near.

*Kelly*

CHAPTER FOUR

# THE PROPOSAL

# DESTINY

I've known her only briefly,
    but I've dreamed of her so long.
I've been waiting half a lifetime
    for her to come along.

She is with me in my solitude
    as I ponder another day.
She has been with me always
    and will never go away.

I've glimpsed her on a busy street
    and in a passing car.
I've never tried to pursue her
    'cause I knew she'd not go far.

And when we finally did meet,
    as on some cosmic cue,
her smiles and laughs and openness
    told me the dream was true.

I've lived for her forever,
    she's affected my whole life.
I've known her only briefly,
    but soon she'll be my wife.

*Kelly*

# PROPOSAL

All my fantasies have paled
    and all my dreams come true.
All my life I've searched to find
    someone just like you.

And now that I have found you
    and have you by my side.
Say that you will stay with me
    through life's long lonely ride.

*Kelly*

# LIFE'S PATH

How narrow the path,
    how straight the gate
How tenuous the course
    of man's fate
How keenly we suffer
    in our strife
How unsubstantial
    our earthly life.

Our future is laid out
    just like a maze
We must not falter
    or lose our ways
We blindly pursue
    our myriad roads
So burdened by
    our tiring loads.

We follow our souls
    to who knows where
Not knowing if
    we'll ever get there
But if we arrive
    with joy and laughter
We'll be together
    forever after.

*Kelly*

# FOXY LADY

Foxy lady, pretty lady,
You fill my days with joy,
I'd swim a mile,
To catch your smile,
And the charm that you employ.

Foxy lady, pretty lady,
My world I want you in,
You touched my soul,
You made me whole,
Life without you would be a sin.

Foxy lady, pretty lady,
I found you, now you're mine,
The you I've known,
The love you've shown,
Confirms what's on my mind.

Foxy lady, pretty lady,
We'll have an exciting life,
Our dreams we'll share,
With passionate flair,
Sweet lady be my wife.

*Karl*

# CHAPTER FIVE

# THE BATTLE GROUND

# BATTLE GROUND

The legendary losers lie
    upon the gory ground.
Their bloody battered bodies die
    and fester all around.

Corrupt decaying corpses sleep
    where once brave men did fight.
Our last farewell to them we weep
    as they greet their eternal night.

*Kelly*

# I DIED

I died a bit to know her
    but I died a lot before
    and it doesn't hurt so very much
    to die a little more.

                *Kelly*

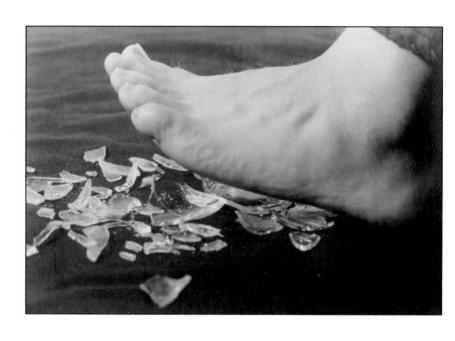

# NIGHTMARE

I dreamed
    I was an alley cat
    fighting for my life,
        but I had no claws.

I dreamed
    I was on a debate team
    in the championship debate,
        but I had laryngitis.

I dreamed
    I made her angry.

*Karl*

# SOMEDAY

I gotta do
I gotta go
This and that
To and fro.

Don't slow down
Keep the pace
Do it now
Don't lose your place.

Things to do
I gotta fly
Get it done
Don't ask me why.

No time now
I gotta run
Someday soon
I'll have some fun.

*Kelly*

# DISAPPOINTMENT

So here we go
      once again,
Together
      hand in hand.

Down the road
      of disappointment,
And yes,
      it's all so grand.

*Karl*

CHAPTER SIX

# THE APOLOGY

# APOLOGY

This is an apology,
      an apology for me,
An apology for the way I am,
      and the way I'll always be.

I'm sorry for the things I say,
      and the things I shouldn't do,
I'm sorry for the world we're in,
      and I'm sorry I love you.

So go ahead and live your life,
      be happy and be free,
Cause this is the last apology
      you'll ever hear from me.

*Kelly*

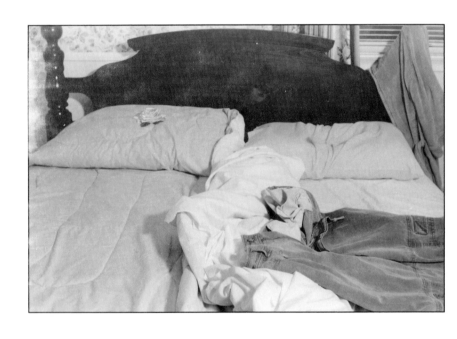

# GROVEL, GROVEL

I dream, not sleep,
I wish, I weep,
All through the lonely night.

My heart, I'll share,
For you, I care,
For you, please let me fight.

I wronged you, again,
I need you, my friend,
Please give me another chance.

Forgive me, now,
I'll change, somehow,
My love, may I have this dance.

.
.
.

I dream, not sleep,
I wish, I weep,
All through the lonely night.

*Karl*

# ANXIOUS

Anxious, anxious, anxious,
My visions swirling around,
My sight a blur,
My thoughts unsure,
My feet not on the ground.

Anxious, anxious, anxious,
My heart is pounding loud,
My chest a-beating,
My breath a-fleeting,
My vitals seem to crowd.

Anxious, anxious, anxious,
My clock is ticking slow,
My time has stopped,
My schedule dropped,
My waiting for the blow.

Anxious, anxious, anxious,
My fears are growing fast,
My mortal sin,
My lady to win,
I pray our love will last.

*Karl*

# WHAT CAN I SAY?

I used to really love you
I used to really care,
I used to really count on you
    and know that you were there.

As the years unfolded
our lives became entwined,
I knew that I was always yours
    and you were always mine.

But now our world has faded
and our love has gone away,
now I don't know who you are
    and I don't know what to say.

*Karl*

# MY MY

My family
My home
That's all I need.

My career
My money
I'm full of greed.

My nerves
My tension
They wrench my neck.

My whiskey
My beer
Say what the heck.

My work
My drinking
They soak up time.

No family
No home
My god-awful crime.

*Karl*

# MY SONG

In the misty twilight dawn,
    all alone, I sing my song
Of fields of wheat, tall and gold,
    and the life that I had but sold.

This room of mine is dull and gray,
    no kind of place to start my day.
My life it seems is just all wrong,
    but I don't care, I've got my song.

The sun creeps over the roof above,
    I sit and dream of the one I love.
She left for good, like on TV,
    and won't be back 'cause now she's free.

The sun is seeping through the shade
    it can shine, I'm not afraid.
Thinking of all that's right and wrong,
    picking my feet and singing my song.

*Kelly*

# LONESOME

I loved you,
I wanted you,
I craved you so.

You loved me,
You wanted me,
You let me go.

I am gone,
I have left,
I am out of here.

You kissed me,
You missed me,
You wished me near.

I was in,
I am out,
You paid the toll.

You knew me,
You freed me,
You lonesome soul.

*Karl*

# BLACK AND WHITE

I guess I've known it
    through the years,
Every smile's
    imbued with tears,
Every laugh
    is fringed with pain,
No love exists
    without a stain.

Our lives will always
    fluctuate
From joy to sorrow,
    love to hate.

But to escape from this,
    our human plight,
This constant change
    from day to night.
To avoid this pit
    of hate and pain,
Don't laugh or smile
    or love again,

But would we be
    so far ahead,
Or would we just
    be almost dead?

*Kelly*

# TODAY

Today I have these problems
    and I hide them very well
I keep them all inside me
    and I start to feel like hell.

Today I have an urging
    and I want to feel good
I don't have any patience
    although I know I should.

Today will be my last time
    I won't do it anymore
Oh my God, here I go
    and it's just like before.

Today I will not do it
    I'll find another way
I know I can be very strong
    and I'll get better every day.

*Karl*

# CHAPTER SEVEN

# ALONE AGAIN

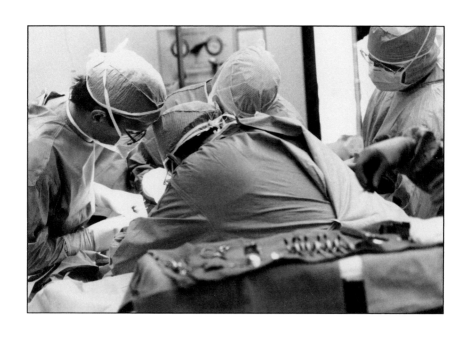

Don't worry about me...

I just wanted to let you know.

I am going in for major surgery this morning.

I'm going to have my heart removed.

# ALONE AGAIN

Three years have now come and gone,
    and life is lonely still,
It seems it's always been that way,
    and I guess it always will.

My fantasies are now gone,
    never to return.
There's no such thing as happiness,
    when will I ever learn.

So down the road I go again,
    walking by myself.
I've packed up all my love and joy,
    and left it on the shelf.

*Kelly*

The darkness of my loneliness

fills the hollow of my life.

*Karl*

# EXCITEMENT

Excitement is the word
Nervous, jumpy, beside myself
A bottle that'll calm my nerves
     sits high upon the shelf.

It's decision time,
Do I make it or...
Do I break it?

It's my future that I contemplate
So for now, I'll just sit.

*Karl*

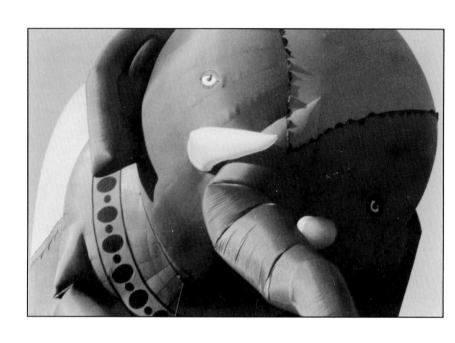

# IF YOU KNOW WHAT I MEAN

The sheep are in the meadow
The mirror is on the wall
The figs are in the fig bowl
The hall is in the hall.

The rubber stamped medallion
In its place beyond the time
Of fire flied bananas ripe
And not knowing what is crime.

The moonstruck shore bonanza
In the barroom slowly brawl
The time to go has come and gone
But snow may never fall.

The moon above the breathless grass
Harks the dreadful bloody scene
The icon blood of many cries...
If you know what I mean.

*Kelly*

# THE CURE

We seem to hurt the ones we love
    although we do not mean to.
We want to say we're sorry
    and that we usually do.

We say it was the last time
    and we say it again and again.
Please listen to what I say
    and do take heed, my friend.

The future is the future
    although you're awful sure.
Never is a long, long time
    and you'll always need the cure.

*Karl*

# I WISH

I wish it was over
I wish it was done
I wish it hadn't started
    but it's only begun.

First the enticement
And then the desire
Now it's the craving
    for strong liquid fire.

*Karl*

# HEAVY

I am heavy and over-burdened
 like an underpowered locomotive.

I am weak and over-challenged
 like a fawn deep in clay mud.

I am alone.

*Karl*

# HOPE

Life is just practice for dying.
Love's just a prelude to crying.
Happiness is fodder for sorrow,
      but things may look better tomorrow.

*Kelly*

CHAPTER EIGHT

# THE PERSONALS

*Kelly*

# THE VERY PERSONALS

Kinda nice,
Kinda shy,
Kinda handsome,
Kinda guy.

Seeking someone,
Kinda sweet,
Kinda pretty,
Kinda neat.

If this is you,
Kindly reply,
Cause I may be
Your kinda guy.

*Kelly*

*Karl*

# GIVE ME A RING

A little crazy,
A little wild,
A lot of humor,
But a little mild.

A little weather,
It's nature's call.
A walk in leaves,
It's in the fall.

Love the music,
Love to dance,
Some conversation,
Some light romance.

If this verse
You'd like to sing,
Pick up the phone,
Give me a ring.

*Karl*

To be continued. . .